MW00875402

Create *Your Own* Good Enough

Stop Comparing and Start Creating!

By Kimberly Williams

The purpose of this book is to encourage readers to be active in creating their best life possible. This is by no means legal, financial nor psychological advice.

Copy © 2018 by Kimberly Williams. All rights reserved.

Published by Kimberly Williams

Cover design by Lulu

ISBN 978-1-387-52357-3

Dedication

This book is dedicated to all those who struggle with the need to be accepted by others in life. I want to help with changing the blueprint of your mind. I also want to dedicate this book to my lovely daughters Destiny-Irisiona and Dajaih-Olivia... I want them to always know that they hold the power within to make life great. So, there is no need to look outside of yourself for that "thing" in life that you think will make you better.

Contents

Introduction

Do you ever find yourself drifting off into deep thought about where you wish you were in life? Then something inside you speaks to you saying, "You're not good enough. You couldn't possibly expect to be successful now. Look at all the bad choices you have made in your life so far." Then the next voice says, "Don't even think about being anything close to what you see in other successful people. You are not pretty, smart or handsome enough to do what they are doing."

Hey! Don't beat yourself up about it. We all have those thoughts at one time or another. Those thoughts will continue to reveal their ugly little faces, but you have to learn to defeat them every time. Trust me, it can be done. You just have to learn to create your own good enough.

Anything You Can Do I Can Too!

1

I will never forget the day I decided that I was good enough to earn my degree. I know to some, college was just a given after finishing high school. It was not that way for me because I never had the life of a "normal" teen girl. I had always done well when I was in school, but going to college just did not seem like an option at the time. After all, I was a single teen mother. I figured I would just work hard and send my daughter to college instead. I was always comparing myself to those who did not get pregnant as a teen and had finished high school, or were at least still attending. Big Mistake!

"Never compare your situation to someone because you think that they are doing so much better than you are. In fact, you just may be doing better. Even if you are not, it really is not what's important. You didn't come into this world to win a race against anyone."

Getting back to my decision to go to college. I was around 19 years old, and a social worker saw something in me that I did not see at the time. He said to me, "Ms. Williams, stop acting as if your life is over just because you have a baby. You're not the only one with a baby. You haven't even began to live yet." I did not want to hear that from him, but he was right. Sometimes all you need is a swift kick in the "you know what" in order to get out of self-pity. Now that I am 37 years young, I know exactly what he was saying. He also went on to say that I would be able to take better care of my baby if I take care of me first. That is so true. Often times as parents, we want the best for our children. However, we can't give them the best if we are not at our best.

I was walking in a park one day just thinking. I said aloud, "I am going to college!" Now of course I didn't know the first thing about how I was going to make this happen. I just knew that I had always wanted to go ever since I could remember. I always wanted to be like the business woman who really had herself together. I especially wanted to be like the attorneys! I loved the brief cases, black suits, and high heeled pumps because, in my mind, they were powerful women. I was so you young and hopeful back in the early 1990s.

Just as I started to think of how I could maybe get into Durham Technical Community

College, there came those crazy voices of doubt again. "How are you going to college? You have a baby and a low paying job. On top of that you live in the projects." Wrong!

Going to college while living in the projects may be the best thing to do. The rent is low, and some pay nothing at all. There is financial aid to help with the tuition and books. Then you sometimes get a refund which can help you in the commute to and from classes. No excuses allowed!

The rebellious, resilience in me just would not let the devil win. I drove my little burgundy Plymouth Acclaim right up to the school. I went straight to admissions and asked for help. I wanted to know how and when I was going to start school. Funny thing is that I didn't know what my major would be at the time.

I chose the paralegal program when I initially enrolled at the community college. The major really didn't make a difference to me at the time because I just wanted to go to college. I changed my major approximately four times, but I was still in school and doing extremely well at it.

A few years later after realizing that the paralegal, professional secretary, office systems, and nursing were not for me. Yes, I had tap danced around all of those majors because I did not know what I wanted to do. I was at a standstill. Before I knew it, I had dropped out of Durham Technical Community College. Soon after, I decided that I needed to get my four year degree. I was now pregnant with my second child. Just to be clear, she was also **my last child**. I was still working on winning the "foolish woman" award at that time, aside from everything else. I digress. As I was saying, I had dropped out of Durham Technical Community College. I knew I still needed to do something, so I enrolled into the Center for Employment Training. There I met my instructor. Ms Deidra Gauze, a very inspirational woman. We called her Ms. D. She taught the Medical Billing course there. I learned quite a bit during the three months that it took to get my certification.

Thinking back, I know she is one of the people who encouraged me to go back to college. My memory during that time was unbelievable. So much to the point that she could not believe just how much information I could retain. She would always say that I needed to put my memory and my expedient learning to higher use. I couldn't see it for myself at first, but soon gained the confidence to believe in my own abilities.

Let Go of the "Tuck ~n~ Roll" Mindset.

2

For once in my life, I could see myself aiming higher. I wanted to do more than what was expected of me. I began to feel that I deserved to get my bachelor degree just as much as any other person. Sometimes we want more, but don't believe that we are good enough to get what it is that we want. Sure I had my doubts and fear when I decided to go for my degree, but I didn't let that stop me from trying. Within three years, I earned my bachelor of science in accounting.

I later got my master's degree in accounting and financial management. I soon found out that accounting can be rather boring after working in corporate America for a few years. None the less, I made a decision that I was good enough to go to college and do well. I did just that. In fact, I did it all while working and being a mother of two lovely daughters.

If you have the will, a way will either present itself or you will need to **_CREATE_** a way. It is up to you to make choices in life to have and do in life the thing that your heart desires. Anything is possible when you set your mind to make it happen.

However, you first have to let go of the old "tuck and roll" mindset. The tuck and roll mindset is when you make a mistake, and you let the negative outcome effect other decisions you make. By doing so, you are giving up on the possibility that things could ever be better. I will give you two prime examples of the tuck and roll syndrome that I have seen with my generation.

Trust that I am not making the following situations up. Of course I am not using any situations to bring shame to anyone. However, foolish loose living happens every day. I'm sure we all know someone who is just throwing their life down the drain. No matter how hard you try to help them, they just keep digging a deeper hole for themselves. Just do your best not to be one of them. It really hits home if the person that is not living up to their potential when it's a relative or very close friend.

A Hot Hell of a Mess!

3

My first example involves a young woman who does not value her body, life, nor her well-being. My second example involves a man who has also given up on life because he has made some life altering mistakes as well. Please note that these are not examples of anyone that I know directly. This book was written to inspire, and not bring shame to anyone I know personally. The examples are just a way to show just how far down a person can go if they fail to be an active participant in taking control of their life.

Alexis gets pregnant at age 16. She soon drops out of high school, and gets a job. The job only paid minimum wage, which was around $5.75 during that time. Alexis knows that chances are she will have to raise her child on her own because the father didn't have much to say when she told him that she was pregnant. No surprise there. He is only seventeen. He is just as irresponsible as she is. So what now?

Nine months later, vulnerable Alexis gives birth to her first baby girl. She has to be out of work for a while, so she receives welfare checks, food stamps, and Medicaid to help with the cost of taking care of a new baby. Alexis is now officially a statistic.

At this point, there is a chance for Alexis to reflect. If she would just make the decision to either abstain from sex or get on birth control, just maybe she could turn her life around for the best. Right? Well it is always easier to say than it is to do. It is my hope that this far into reading that you will recognize the "branch" in which she could have grabbed onto to change her life. But no... She does just the opposite. She tucks and rolls a little more.

She soon meets another guy and falls for him almost instantly. She gave herself to him, and is now pregnant with her second. By now her first baby is only one year old. Alexis is about to give birth again, and she is not even 18 years old. She is barely able to take care of the first baby. There is no baby daddy in sight, so she is left to be a baby momma all alone. Not cool.

Why does this happen? What was she thinking? This could have been prevented had she been on birth control, or abstained from sex altogether. But hey! Who hasn't made a mistake or two in life by failing to do what we know is right to prevent unwanted consequences? The thing is to be able to recognize and put a stop to the mess before things go too far.

Seven babies later, Alexis has an epiphany. *Seven?!* Yes, I said seven! She now realizes that she has spent most of her youth being pregnant. You may be wondering what took her so long to see that she was not making the best choices by having so many children. She has no husband, an 8th grade education, and now she has all of those mouths to feed. Shouldn't she have known better by the time she had the third baby?

It can be so easy to pass judgment when you know nothing about a person's mental state. The real issue is that she fell into the *tuck and roll* trap, and failed to reach out and grab a branch on her way down to pull herself up.

I know you're probably saying to yourself, "What the heck would be her branch?" Um let's see. Her branch would have been birth control, condoms, or abstinence. However, it does not matter what you say about the situation. Until a person decides that they are good enough to be treated as something more than a "jump off", they will continue to tuck and roll.

Alexis has to start with the renewing of her mind. In order to do something different or better, you have to change the way that you think first. Everything starts with a thought. Yes. Even you and I were first a thought before we were manifested into to life's creation. There is nothing that you can do, and do it well if you do not change your mind set if it is already negative.

One has to change the blueprint in their mind. Your thoughts create actions so you have to create a new way of thinking. If you feel you can't create a new way of thinking, borrow a new way of thinking. It can't be much worse than the thinking that got you to where you are now.

In relation to Alexi's situation, we all know that although men have a part in getting a woman pregnant, they do not actually give birth. Therefore, I will use another example for men to relate. This does not excuse the role that the man plays in the situation. But as women, we have to value our precious divine power of the "V." It starts with us.

Don't Tuck ~n~ Roll John!

4

Now let's talk about "John's" dilemma.
Oh you know I could not forget to tell you
about this one. John is now 30 years old and
living with his mother. He never did the
mental transition from a boy to a man. He is
finding it hard to get a job that pays him
enough to commit his time.

As an entrepreneur, I can sure enough
reason with John in some ways. Our time is
important, but baby boy is going about it in
the wrong way. He did find a job eventually.
However, he only worked long enough to buy
product to become a "street pharmacist." For
those who are wondering. A street pharmacist
is slang used to describe a drug dealer. John

decided to sell drugs as a quick way to make money.

We all know that all money is not good money. I could be wrong. Ummm...Let's see. It all spends the same. Yes! However, sometimes the way you make the money will do you more harm than good. So you know how the story goes. John gets caught selling drugs, and is put in jail. Not only does John go to jail, but now his mom kicks him out of the house. She does not want her drug hustling son living with her, nor does she want the drama that comes along with drugs. Wow! Talk about going downhill.

John is finally released from jail after a very short time. He is offered to participate in a program that is free, and will help him find work. He refused the program because there were just too many rules that he did not want to follow. DAMN IT!!! John didn't grab the branch. Instead, he tucked and rolled! The program would have been the branch that he could have used to keep himself from going further and further down in life. Sadly enough, John ended up going back to jail for a longer period of time. He is now getting older, and has two felony charges on his record.

Hold on! This does not mean that his life is over. There are people who are extremely successful in spite of their run in with the law. John can turn his situation around if he changes his mindset. What we don't need is for John to begin to feel worthless because of his mistakes.

John now needs to figure out his purpose for being on earth. We were all placed here for a reason. We have a purpose, but some just find it harder than others to realize what the purpose is. It could be that John is an entrepreneur who needs a life coach. We as a people need not to write him off. Regardless of what society thinks, John now has to create his own "good enough" if he wants a better life.

Both characters described previously need not to worry themselves with what the outsiders say they are worth. They have to create their own "good enough." I caution you! In creating your own good enough, be careful not to set your standards too low. Aim as high as your imagination will carry you. Don't base your goals or standards on what you think others expect from you. You will fail every time if you do. Remember they probably expect you to fail anyway.

You have to get into a state of certainty, and decide that no matter how bad you think you are right now, you will not let it stop you from seeking better for yourself. You may not be able to even stand to look in the mirror right now at yourself. Guess what! No one who is honest with themselves can say that they have never done anything that is considered bad. We all have. By now it's just a case of so the heck what!

What are you going to do about it? Are you going to continue to beat yourself up for your past? Yes, it is the past. If you didn't do it today, in this present moment in time, **IT IS THE PAST!** Let it go and stop double jeopardizing yourself. You committed the crime or the bad deed years, weeks, or even days ago, and you've paid for it. Yet, you keep punishing yourself with the same torment repeatedly. Come on loves!!! You deserve to treat yourself so much better than that.

No Need to Compete

5

You have to stop looking around and comparing yourself. Stop doing everything possible in order to appear in the sight of others to be on the right track, when all the while you are perpetrating a useless front. Instead, you should be looking for ways to live your life as the character you were born to be. Not the character that society has cast you out to be.

Ask for help beloved. Find a mentor or someone that you admire. You would be amazed at how many people who are doing well, and want to reach back and help the next person. If I did it, I know you can. I was a high school dropout, pregnant by age fifteen, and gave birth at sixteen. I didn't have so much as a tiny pot to piss in. I sure as hell didn't have a window to throw it out of. I did not let that stop me, and you shouldn't either. Don't let your past, or even who you are today, stop you. Be grateful that you have a chance to do something about it now, and face it head on. Every day that you show up on this earth alive, you have an opportunity to do something about your situation.

I will share with you the one thing that I did that really helped me. *MOTIVATIONAL SPEAKERS!!!* Some refer to themselves as life coaches. Motivational speakers you say? Yep!

There are two speakers *(Les Brown and Bob Proctor)* who I began to listen to daily. I listen to Les Brown because I believe we both have a little of the same kind of "crazy" in us. I listen to Bob Proctor because we share some of the same ideas about making money. We both believe that working a job for someone else is not the best way to earn money long-term.

There are many others that I listen to as well. However, I only listen to those who are providing messages that relate to the kind of life that I am creating for myself. I can't tell you which ones you should listen to because that's up to you. It will depend on what you are trying to create for your life.

I will tell you this. You should listen to the older greats, and new speakers such as myself; take some of what you learn and put it to use. Trust that your life will never be the same. Let your mind get involved because we will interrupt the daunting story in your head that you believe about yourself.

The one reason that I became a public speaker is because it is a way for me to help others break free. To this day, I am highly motivated in life awareness speaking.

Listening to speakers, and being able to talk to them in person is a lot more life changing than just sitting around reading self-help books most times. However, if you can't get to them by all means read the books! Get the information in your subconscious mind as soon as possible. Faith comes by hearing something over and over again. You will remember more of what you hear on a regular basis than what you read. You already have the proof.

Some of us can still remember the negative things that was said almost ten years ago. That is because we began to believe what we hear. Hearing all of the negativity over the years from family, stranger, and so called friends will cause you to have faith in what they say to you. Yes it's negative, but you really start to believe it. It's evident in the way that you live your life now. So many subliminal messages have been embedded in the subconscious mind for so long.

There is a nest egg of negative messages that are sitting there waiting to hatch every second. I am no stranger to the little birds that hatch and begin to sing the chorus to discouraging songs. They sing songs like "You're Never Going to Make It"... "You Suck At everything" and "Why Can't You Just Live like Everyone Else"...and so on and so forth. I know those are some pretty awful songs to hear playing in your head, so I have a question for you. What are you going to do to change those songs to more positive and upbeat songs?

One thing I would advise you to do is to rid yourself of people who speak negativity into your life. Surround yourself with people who say and do things to encourage you. This will interrupt the messages that you already have in your mind about who you are and what you are capable of.

Began to create a new reality for yourself. I say this because you are the only one who can decide to do more and have more. The life coach will be there to help you along the way, but you have to take action. For once in your life, make the decision that you are good enough to at least do that. Believe you are worth more than what you have experienced thus far.

Stop Comp Thinking.

6

I just want you to understand that the messages that are in your mind are what's effecting your ability to have success. What is success anyway? It is accomplishing whatever goals or plan of action that you have set out to do. I had to do three things in order to get my mind right to attract success to me.

First, I had to let go of what I like to call "*comp thinking*." Comp thinking is when you look at yourself and your situation and compare it to everyone else around you. It's like what real estate agents do with houses. They do comparisons to see how one property measures up to the surrounding properties. Guess what!!! We are not real estate! We don't have to compare ourselves to others in order to determine our worth.

The second thing I did was I begin to seek and listen to positive messages daily about retraining your brain. I have learned that you can change any situation by changing your mental wiring. This is true in almost anything.

For example, if you want to lose weight, change the way you think about food. Begin to think of food as nourishment for your body, and not something you eat for comfort. Stop eating when you are not hungry. How many times have we all eaten because it's a certain time of day without even being hungry? Some of us eat around noon just because it is known to be "lunch time"...but why? What if you are still full from breakfast and don't really need to eat? Do you just eat anyway because that is what the majority is doing? If so, STOP IT! Do some self-evaluating to figure out what times of the day is best for you to eat, according to how your body reacts to food.

Another example would be if you want better relationships with people, you may need to make some changes. First, change the way you think about yourself. After you do that, then you should pay close attention to how you feel when around those people. It may be that you should change the way you think about people. Are you spending precious time worrying if people like you?

My next example is about that mighty dollar! If you want to keep money, think of it as a tool and not as a means to just buy stuff... just to keep up with the folk you see on "Bravo TV."

The third thing is, I wrote a schedule for daily activities that I need to complete on a daily basis. They were basic but were very detailed in description. I wrote down what time I would get up in the mornings. I wrote down what I would do as soon as I got up. I mean I really wrote down everything that I knew would be a part of my day. This will help to keep your mind from wandering, and allow your brain to focus.

Random thoughts come into our heads at a more rapid pace when we are out of focus. I am speaking from experience. I see the difference in me when I am not sticking to a schedule. I begin to feel a little depression coming on. I begin to feel as if I know I should be doing something to work on my goals.

When you are working on something that will improve or enhance your life, you just feel different. It's a good different! The negative thoughts are quieted by the thoughts of the possibilities because it is then that we have hope.

You see, success is a mind thing. Success does not discriminate. It doesn't judge you based on how you look, what you have done in your past, nor how much money you don't have. You already have what you need inside of you to do what you desire to do.

Keep the Momentum Going!

7

Now that you have made up your mind to grab hold of that branch, it's time to take action. You have made the decision to get out of the tuck and roll zone. So now I have one question for you. What are you going to do stay motivated to create your own good enough?!

Now I am sure this is the part of the book where many writers would make an honest attempt to give you a step by step method to follow. Well that would be the most dishonest thing that a person could do for you when you are trying to create your own destiny. I say this because it's all about creating YOUR own good enough. What's good for me, may not be what is best for the next person.

How could anyone possibly know your good enough if they have never lived your life? The *good enough* is not some cookie cutter instruction, or a one size fits all type deal. Instead, it is about individuals becoming comfortable in their own skin. We don't have to reconstruct ourselves in order to fit in someone else's skin. The skin you were born in is quite all right.

What I will do is tell you what I have done, and am still doing to this day. But first I had to get real clear about what is good enough for me. What will get me to the point where I can say that I am truly maximizing my potential to be the best me possible?

Then I asked myself what really matters to me in life. I soon figured out that my interest are not the everyday run of the mill desires.

I have <u>no</u> desire to have a big house with a white picket fence, a dog, and a couple of toddlers playing in the yard. For one, I don't ever want to own any pets, and my daughters are not babies anymore. I love my daughters, and would not dare have another baby. Yes I am still young enough to do so, but it's just not my thing. Furthermore, I do not like the appearance of a white picket fence. Ha! I guess I am just weird that way.

Give me a deluxe apartment in the sky in a beautiful downtown metro area with no yard, and I am great! That is beside the point I know, but I am just demonstrating that we do not all want the same things.

We do not all need to look alike either. So if you compare your appearance to that of others, and then get depressed about it STOP IT! Decide on how you want to dress, live, eat, pray, and love. Do things on your own terms because truthfully that is the only way you will ever feel good enough.

For example, I don't keep up with the latest fashion because I will wear something whether it is in season or not. It is not that I am such an outcast. It is simply that I refuse to march to the beat of somebody else's drum. I create my own music and will dance to it however I see fit. The trend is not relevant when you live your life in absolute certainty.

It's hard to really feel good about yourself if you are the kind of person who goes whichever way the wind blows. Find out what really matters to you no matter what is going on in the world around you.

I know there are many distractions that may keep us from focusing on self. Every time you turn on your television, you will see what media says about the way we should look, dress, and act in order to be considered good enough.

Let's not forget that a lot of us are using Facebook to communicate. How many times have you logged onto your page only to see quotes about beauty? You see images of men and women basically competing to be the most like for their appearance.

They want to be liked for being able to afford the most expensive clothes. The women want to be liked for having the biggest bottom, and the smaller waist. Men want to be liked for having the most SWAGG. Whatever that really means.

Anyway, I want you to understand why it is that most do this. They want to feel GOOD ENOUGH!!! That is a life of quiet desperation in my opinion. It would be so much better not to have to depend on the validation from Facebook friends, also known as strangers. I am really hoping you are feeling me on this one.

I am sure we have all felt the need to be accepted by other people at one time or another. IT really becomes a problem when it consumes you. When you develop an obsession with pleasing others, and you forget about what you really want that's when it becomes a serious problem.

It's Just T.V. Folks!

8

Oh my Lord, please! Let me address the issue with trying to live up to what we see on television. I am seeing too many people trying to be a carbon copy of someone else. That is definitely a hot mess going somewhere fast to sure enough happen!

Please realize that you don't have to look like a celebrity in order to be beautiful or handsome. Heck, they don't even look like themselves. Photoshop, makeup (even on men), weaves, and surgery will make the most unattractive person look more appealing to the untrained eye.

What ever happened to being unique? Why would you want to look like someone who on a regular basis doesn't look like what you see on television or in the magazines? Be for real! Do you think people really walk around in costume all day? It is simply entertainment.

Meanwhile, here we are walking around in the local Wal-Mart and such with pink wigs on, and unreasonably high heels. Our men are walking around with unnecessary amounts of costume jewelry in order to appear to be "balling." I know that is the incorrect spelling, but that's how folks say it. Give me a break! That has nothing to do with creating your own good enough or being yourself. Well let me just say that it is not being your authentic self.

Another thing I have to address is some of our up and coming artists. I am speaking to this audience because I am definitely an artist as well. I know that success leaves clues. Yes.

This is true. However, this does not mean we need another Nicki Minaj, nor do we need a plethora of Lil Wayne copy cats running around either. Who you are is enough as an artist, or just as a person in general. In fact, you would probably reach success at a faster rate if you can just do your own thing.

Give us something fresh! What you have is good enough. I know that I have repeated this several times throughout this book. That is because I seriously want you to get the idea, that you are good enough, into your subconscious mind.

Understand that God did not make a mistake when he allowed you to manifest into to a living and breathing creature on this earth. Everything from the first hair that you've ever grown from your scalp on down to the crust at the bottom of your feet. You are one of His most phenomenal creations. It may be that you just need a little convincing. That is exactly what will happen if you take what I am saying as truth serum.

Beware of Wolves Disguised as Do-Gooders

9

It would be unfair if me not to warn you about the "wolves!" Those are the people who see that you are doing well, or at least trying. Then they come into your life pretending to want to help you when all the while they are just in it to see what they can get by riding your coat tail. I know it sounds crazy, but it is the truth.

As you begin to create your own "good enough," you may find that you become very popular with stranger for the wrong reasons. You've started to work on yourself. Things are now looking up for you, and they can see it for you! Then someone magically shows up in your life out of the blue.

Well let me tell you how it happened to me. If you know me by now, I can always provide a true story for the advice that I give to you beloved.

It had been almost one year since I published my first book, "No Longer Ugly Inside." Things were going pretty good. Not phenomenal, but I had something there. I revamped my Facebook page so that I could expand to other people in other cities. I figured I had better create my own way since I was not getting much publicity as a local author in North Carolina.

All of a sudden, I am getting more support for my book. I decided that my book was more than just a book. It is a movement that I needed more people to know about. Well I got exactly what I asked for as far as more notice for my efforts. However, I also attracted to me a "Do-Gooder." This guy pursued me as if I announced that I'd won the lottery. He was relentless.

I mean seriously… this dude contacted me asking if he could fly into North Carolina from another state to have lunch with me. He claimed that he wanted to discuss the possibilities of him helping me with getting more exposure for the NLUI Movement that I was creating with my book.

Now of course my "bull shit" alarm began to sound, but I ignored it. I said, "Hey, what do I have to lose?" How about my sanity? Ha! Anyways, this dude caught a flight in from Atlanta that following week. I should have known that he was a bit too eager to meet me. Long story short, he was just someone who saw how much attention that I was stirring up and he wanted to be a part of it.

He was only out to see what he could get from me. He wanted me to help him with some projects that he was not doing well with, and get more attention for his consulting business. I helped him for a little while until I realized that he was trying too hard to be a part of all of my endeavors. This man even went so far as to pretend that he wanted to be in a relationship with me. He pretended to be so attracted to me. Lucky for me, I wised up before anything detrimental to my success could happen. He even asked to be a part of a cleaning company that I was planning to start at that time. Really dude? How greedy can one person be? I am so glad that we never signed any agreement because his intentions were selfish and misguided. God was truly watching out for me as always! Thank you Lord.

Please don't let my story stop you from accepting help when you're on your journey to creating your path. Just be careful, and be mindful of the fake "do-gooders!" The fake ones will have you to believe that it's all about you. When all the while they are simply trying to ride with you just to get their business or venture exposure.

Needless to say, I cut that so called relationship right at the knees. It was over before it started. God is not going to let you prey on His children for long. Before you know it. He will step in and take control. He will most certainly speak to you, but it is up to you to listen to what He is saying to you. I am not trying to preach to you, but know that what I am saying is real. I could have ended up really getting plaid by this fool, but instead I had the sense to cut the ties and move on.

Don't Just Grow Old.

10

Get better with age. Learn to embrace growing older. It is definitely a blessing. This does not mean that you need to stop living, enjoying life, and having fun. No, not at all.

When I say get better with age, I am simply saying that you don't have to try to pretend to be something that you are not. I see so many men and women who are just not living in a way that will complement who they are in reference to where they truly are in the lifespan development cycle. Not to get too deep into any psychological content, but it's real.

Let's just talk about a few examples. Karen is a 39 year old attractive and fit African American woman, with three teenaged daughters. She has been divorced for a little over six years. Karen is beginning to feel the effects of growing older. She just can't put her finger on it, but something about here just feels different. She just does not feel as beautiful and desired as she did a few years ago.

Hey now! You may be thinking that it is absolutely normal for Karen to have these feelings. You are absolutely right! However, let me explain Karen's actions as she tries to get her "youth" back. You see, Karen is looking around at all of the new beauties on the scene. She was use to going out places and being the center of the attention when she was younger. Now she is feeling like the old chick in the room. So what does Karen decide to do? She begins to dress differently. I mean different in a bad way.

She purposely goes out and buys everything she can afford that the 16 to 21 year old young ladies are wearing. She went platinum blonde. Which really just made her look like a street walker. Let's be real. Blonde hair does not look good on everyone...in my opinion. OK! Karen is one of those people. Then she started to get those crazy designs on her nails like the teens do. I mean a different color on each fingernail, with a different design as well. Her skirts are entirely too short. Lord knows her shirts dip too low as well. You can darn near see the areolas on her breast. That's just how low cut the shirts are. There is nothing wrong with Karen wanting to crank up her sexy, but there is such a thing as having a little class with it.

On top of dressing like a street walking mishap, she is now back into clubbing almost every freaking weekend. Seriously?! She got tired of being single and not feeling desired, so she starts dating a guy who just made 21. Could she get any crazier? Yes, she really could. I am not making this up. There are really women who are living Karen's testimony.

The problem I have the most with everything about Karen that I just mentioned is the fact that she is the mother of teens. Those teens are going to see their mother trying to be something she's not. Karen may be at risk for losing their respect along with her dignity.

That is just a real example of what not being happy with who you are can do for you. Karen was not happy with growing older, so she tried to be something she is not. What she should have done, was reinvent herself. I am not saying that just because a person gets older that they should lose all sex appeal, and curl up and die. Just know, when you look as if you are trying way too hard to get attention, you will get attention. I am sure of it, but all attention is not to be desired. Do you not want to be respected? You are a woman now. You are not some little girl wondering aimlessly. Don't be the one who seeks attention from anyone with a pair of fairly functioning eyeballs.

Reinventing yourself is totally different from dressing up in costume, and hoping to reverse the hands of time. I don't care how many colors, makeup, nails, and short skirts you put on. You will still be just a middle aged woman dressed in junior attire. Not cool. Why try to look like a spring chicken, when you are a more like a fine wine. You really can get better with age.

A lot of women, who had children in their younger years, are finding that they now have more time to take care of self. Now the children are older. The older you become, you should be more comfortable in your skin because you began to get a real sense of who you are. That is provided you are progressing mentally and spiritually as we should.

I am not as old as Karen yet, but I will be there soon enough. My advice to my future self would be to embrace the woman I have become. Please don't try to be 21 again. Instead, embrace the beauty in aging gracefully. Yes, it is definitely a great thing to have fun! I will probably have more fun than in my earlier years because I would be more stable mentally, spiritually, and most certainly financially.

Men go through it too. You will see some get their fancy new fast cars. Some will even trade their car for a motorcycle. LOL! Now that is funny to me, but I am not here to judge. I have heard folks say in those situations that they are going through a mid-life crisis.

Yes, some men do go through times when they wish they could get back those youthful years. You ever see the man who is darn near 50 trying to act like he is 25? I have. I almost married one. Ha! Thank the Lord I dodged that deadly bullet! You ever stop to think why that is? He has not yet figured out how to reinvent himself.

He thinks it would be easier to play a con game while being a complete fraud. It's a sad sight to see because they are really missing out on the pure freedom of being just who they are supposed to be.

Pretending to be someone else is not the same as creating your own good enough. Nope, that is trying to be someone else's good enough because you are no longer in that space. Accept it! Love it! Embrace it, and get on with creating your new life. One that resonates with where you are in life now. Be in the now. Create in the now.

Your life will begin to be so good that you will just want to hug yourself. I know I do. The more I start to live the way that I want to live, the more I love who I am. When I am living in a space that I am not the creator of, I am not in balance. Life should and can be an awesome and exciting journey if you make it that way. So, please do yourself and the Universe a favor... CREATE *YOUR OWN* GOOD ENOUGH!!!

"Never tuck and roll again. Instead grab on to a branch when you're going downhill, and get back up again. It is then that you can begin to create your own good enough"
-Kimberly Williams

Self-Reflecting Questions

- Are you living your best life?

  _____
  _____
  _____
  _____
  _____
  _____

- If not, what are you going to do about it?

  _____
  _____
  _____
  _____
  _____
  _____

- What changes can you make today to get you closer to your dreams?

  _____
  _____
  _____
  _____
  _____
  _____

If you answered the previous three questions, you are now at least one step closer to creating a new you. Now get busy living!

Made in the USA
Middletown, DE
05 February 2023

24094504R00040